Percentages for life and work

Learn practical business maths that you can actually use!

What this short book is all about

- Introduction (why percentages, why do you need them?)
- Percentages as fractions
- Percentages as decimals
- Quick percentage tips
- Working out percentages
- Percentage increase and decrease
- Percentage change
- Reverse percentages
- Practical percentages: discounts
- Practical percentages: value added tax (vat) / sales tax
- Practical percentages: income tax
- Practical percentages: simple interest
- Practical percentages: compound interest
- Summary and recap

Inside the book

- Each section explains one topic
- One example to show you how to work out
- One task for you to try (with answers, don' t worry)

1: Introduction to percentages

Why percentages?

- Have you ever bought something?
- You probably paid a sales tax or value added tax (vat).
- That's a percentage of the cost.
- What about saving money?
- Interest is worked out as a percentage.

Where percentages are used?

- Work out increases/decreases, e.g. salary increase, inflation
- Work out sales tax or value added tax?
- Work out discounts
- Work out interest on your money

What are percentages?

- Percent means out of 100
- Symbol is %
- 100% of something = the whole amount

24% (24 out of 100) - shaded

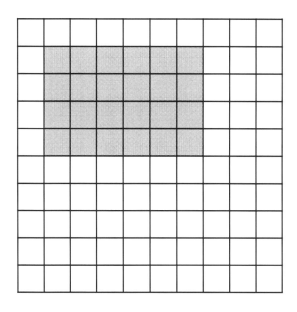

What are percentages task

Percent means out of:

a) 10
b) 100
c) 1000

Answer is: b, percent is out of 100.

2: Percentages as fractions

Percentages as fractions

- 11% means 11 out of 100
- As a fraction, this is $\dfrac{11}{100}$
- 20 % means 20/100
- As a fraction this is:

- $\dfrac{20}{100} = \dfrac{2}{10}$ (divide top and bottom by 10)

- $\dfrac{2}{10} = \dfrac{1}{5}$ (divide top and bottom by 2)

Percentages to fractions task

- Convert 25% to a fraction

Answer

$$\frac{25}{100} = \frac{5}{20} \text{ (divide by 5)} = \frac{1}{4} \text{ (divide by 5)}$$

Fractions to percentages

- To change a fraction into a percentage, multiply by 100.

Example

Write $\frac{3}{5}$ as a percentage

Answer

$$\frac{3}{5} \times 100 = \frac{300}{5} = 60\%$$

Fractions to percentages task

Question:

Write $\frac{2}{5}$ as a percentage

Answer

$\frac{2}{5} \times 100 = \frac{200}{5} = 40\%$

3: Percentages as decimals

Percentages as decimals

- To change a percentage to a decimal, divide by 100.
- Work out 11% as a decimal
- 11% = $\frac{11}{100}$ = 0.11

Percentages to decimals task

- Convert 25% to a decimal

Answer

$$\frac{25}{100} = 0.25$$

Decimals to percentages

- To change a decimal into a percentage, multiply by 100.

Example

Write 0.23 as a percentage

Answer

$0.23 \times 100 = 23\%$

Decimals to percentages task

Question:

Write 0.4 as a percentage

Answer

$0.4 \times 100 = 40\%$

4: Quick percentage calculation tips

Percentage tips

- To find 1%, divide by 100
- To find 10%, divide by 10
- To find 20%, divide by 10, then double your answer
- To find 50%, divide by 2

Percentage calculations example: 50%

- Work out 50% of 60

- Answer:
- $60 \div 2 = 30$

Percentage calculations example: 20%

- Work out 20% of 60

Answer:

- Work out 10% first
- $60 \div 10 = 6$
- Double it: 6 x 2 = 12

Percentage calculations task: 5%

- Work out 5% of 60

Answer:

- Work out 10% first
- $60 \div 10 = 6$
- Halve it: $6 \div 2 = 3$

5: Working out percentages

Work out one quantity as a percentage of another

- To work out one quantity as a percentage of another, do this

$$\frac{first\ quantity}{second\ quantity} \times 100$$

Example: Work out 6 as a percentage of 24

Answer

First divide 6 by 24 = $\frac{6}{24}$

Simplify: $\frac{6}{24} = \frac{1}{4}$ (divide top and bottom by 6)

Multiply the answer by 100: $\frac{1}{4}$ x 100 = 25%

Work out percentages task

- Work out 8 as a percentage of 160

Answer

- $\dfrac{8}{160} = \dfrac{2}{40}$ (divide by 4) $= \dfrac{1}{20}$

- $\dfrac{1}{20} \times 100 = 5\%$

6: Percentage increase and decrease

Percentage increase and decrease

- If an amount increases, it goes up.
- If an amount decreases, it goes down.

Example: Increase 90 by 10%

Answer

Divide by 10: 90/10 = 9 (Remember the quick percentage calculation tips)

New amount: 90 + 9 = 99

Percentage decrease task

Decrease 80 by 20%

Answer

Divide by 10: 80/10 = 8 (Remember the quick percentage calculation tips)

20%, so double it : 8 x 2 = 16

New amount: 80 – 16 = 64

7: Percentage change

Percentage change

- To work out percentage change, do this:

Percentage change = $\dfrac{actual\ change}{original\ value} \times 100$

Example: A trader buys a mobile phone cover for $5 and sells it for $8. What is his percentage profit?

Answer

Actual change = $8 - $5 = $3

Original value = $5

Percentage profit = $\dfrac{3}{5} \times 100 = \dfrac{300}{5} = 60\%$

Percentage change task

The number of people in a small village voting for the Monster Loony Raving party rose from 20 to 25 at the last election. What percentage increase is that?

Answer

Actual change = 25 − 20 = 5

Original value = 20

Percentage increase = $\frac{5}{20} \times 100 = \frac{1}{4} \times 100 = 25\%$

(5/20 = ¼ by dividing top and bottom by 5)

8: Reverse Percentages

How to work out reverse percentages

- A trader sells gift items with a 10% discount. Victoria buys a gift item for $9. How much does the original gift item cost?

Answer

Discount price = Normal price less 10% = 100 − 10 = 90%

So 90% of normal price is $9

1% of normal price is $9/90 = $0.1

100% of normal price is 100 x 1% = 100 x $0.1 = $10

Reverse percentages task

Sally gets a 5% pay rise. Her new pay is now $1260 per month. Work out Sally's pay before the rise.

Answer

New pay = old pay + 5% = 100% + 5% = 105%

105 % of old pay = $1260

1% of old pay = $1260/105 = $12

100% of old pay = 100 x 12 = $1200.

9: Practical percentages - discounts

Discounts

- Discounts are amounts taken off the price of an item, often during a sale.
- Discounts are often offered as percentages.
- Remember to subtract!

Example: A blouse costing £30 is discounted by 15%. What is the new price?

Answer

Discount = 15% of £30 = $\frac{15}{100} \times 30 = 0.15 \, x \, 30 =$ 4.5

New price = £30 - £4.5 = £25.50

Discounts task

Jane wants to print some cards and sees this offer:

300 Business Cards
Normal price £25
60% off

Work out the new price:

Answer

Discount = 60% of £25 = $\dfrac{60}{100} \times 25 = 0.6 \; x \; 25 = 15$

New price = £25 - £15 = £10

10: Practical percentages -value added task (Vat)

Value added tax (VAT)

- Some countries charge a percentage of the price of some goods and services and this is paid to the government.

- It is often referred to as value added task (vat) or sales tax.

Example: VAT in the UK is charged at 20%. Use this to work out the VAT on a TV costing £350.

Answer

Actual VAT = 20% x 350 = $\frac{20}{100}$ x 350 = £70

Value added tax task

VAT in a country is charged at 15%. Use this to work out the price inclusive of VAT on a item costing $300.

Answer

VAT = 15% x 300 = $\frac{15}{100}$ x 300 = $45

Price + VAT = $300 + $45 = $345

11: Practical percentages - income tax

About income tax

- Income tax is a percentage of your income that your employer deducts and gives to the government

- The government allows you a tax-free allowance first and the rest is taxed using the income tax percentage.

- Income tax is a bit more complicated than this simple explanation as it often occurs in bands.

- Example: First $10,000 tax free, next $20,000 income tax at 10%, next $50,000 income tax at $20% etc.

Income tax example

A country has a tax free allowance of $10,000 and charges a flat rate of income tax of 12% for any amount above that.   Jane earns $30,000 per year. Work out her income tax and take home pay.

Answer

Tax free = $10,000

Taxable income = $30,000 - $10,000 = $20,000

Income tax = 12% x 20,000 = $\frac{12}{100} \times 20{,}000 = \$2400$

Sally's take home pay: $30,000 - $2,400 = $27,600

Income tax task

A country has the following tax system:

Amount	Income Tax
First $10,000	0
Next $20,000	10%
Above $30,000	20%

Jane earns $40,000.   Work out her income tax.

Answer

Tax free = $10,000

Next $20,000, 10% : Tax = 20,000/10 = $2,000

Above $30,000 = $40,000 – $30,000 = $10,000

Tax: 20% x $10,000

Work out 10% 10,000/10 = $1000, double it = $2,000

Total tax: $2000 + $2000 = $4,000

12: Practical percentages - simple interest

Work out simple interest

- When you save money in a bank or similar institution, you get paid a small percentage of that money as interest.
- With simple interest, the interest is paid out each year and not added to your account.

Simple interest = Amount invested x Time in years x Interest Rate

Example: Adama saves $500 in a bank that pays out interest of 6%. How much interest is paid to Adama after 1 year.

Answer

Simple interest: 6% of 500 = $\frac{6}{100}$ x 1 x 500 = $30

Simple interest task

Question: Adama saves $500 in a bank that pays out interest of 6%. How much interest is paid to Adama after 6 months?

Answer

Amount invested = $500

Time in years = 6/12 = 0.5

Interest rate = 6%

Simple interest: 6% of 500 = $\frac{6}{100}$ x 0.5 x 500 = $15

13: Practical percentages - compound interest

Work out compound interest

- With compound interest, the interest is paid out each year and added to your account.
- This new amount is used to calculate, next years interest.
- Here is a recap of simple interest.

Simple interest = Amount invested x Time in years x Interest Rate

Compound interest example

Work out the total amount in the bank after two years on $100 invested at 5%

Answer

Interest after 1st year: $100 \times 1 \times \dfrac{5}{100} = \$5$

Money after year 1 = $100 + $5 = $105

Interest after 2nd year : $105 \times 1 \times \dfrac{5}{100} = \$5.25$

Money in the bank at the end of the 2nd year: $105 + $5.25 = $110.25

Compound interest task

Work out the compound interest paid out after two and a half years on $100, invested at 5%

Answer

½ a year = 0.5 years

Interest after 1st year: $100 \times 1 \times \dfrac{5}{100} = \$5$

Money after year 1 = $100 + $5 = $105

Interest after 2nd year : $105 \times 1 \times \dfrac{5}{100} = \$5.25$

Money in the bank at the end of the 2nd year: $105 + $5.25 = $110.25

Interest after ½ year in 3rd year : $110.25 \times 0.5 \times \dfrac{5}{100} = \$2.75$

Total compound interest paid: $5 + $5.25 + $2.75 = $13

14: Percentages summary

You have learnt:

- How to work out percentages
- The relationship between percentages, decimals and fractions
- How to work out percentage change
- How to work out percentage increase
- Practical use of percentages to work out:
  - Discounts
  - VAT
  - Income tax
  - Simple and Compound interest

Printed in Great Britain
by Amazon

70933477R00035